COURAGEOUS LEADERS
SINGLE PARENTS
REDEFINING ENTREPRENEURSHIP

COURAGEOUS LEADERS
SINGLE PARENTS
REDEFINING ENTREPRENEURSHIP

Dionne Marie

Dionne Marie Signature Haute Ventures

California

Copyright © 2024 Dionne Marie Flynn
All rights reserved. Printed in the United States of America. No part of this book may be used or reproduced in any manner whatsoever without written permission. For information, send your letters of inquiry to: Dionne Marie Signature Haute Ventures, 2102 Business Center Dr., Suite 130-784, Irvine, CA 92612.

Cover by Dionne Marie

ISBN: 9798328970099

First Edition: June 2024

CONTENTS

DEDICATION 9

ACKNOWLEDGMENTS 11

IMPORTANT NOTE 13

PRAYER 15

SECTION 1 19
    CHAPTER 1: THE VISION 21
    CHAPTER 2: THE COMMITMENT 25
    CHAPTER 3: THE OPPORTUNITY 31

SECTION 2 37
    CHAPTER 4: THE EMBRACE 39
    CHAPTER 5: THE IMPLEMENTATION 45
    CHAPTER 6: THE ADVANCEMENTS 51

SECTION 3 55
    CHAPTER 7: THE LEGALITIES 57
    CHAPTER 8: THE SUSTAINABILITY 61
    CHAPTER 9: THE CRISIS 67

SECTION 4 73
    CHAPTER 10: THE LEGACY 75
    CHAPTER 11: THE FUTURE 79
    CHAPTER 12: THE ETHICS 85
    CHAPTER 13: THE QUESTIONS 87

SECTION 5 91
    CHAPTER 14: THE SINGULARITY 93
    THE AUTHOR'S STORY 99

DEDICATION

This book is dedicated to my daughter, son, grandchildren and all the single parents out there rubbing together two sticks to keep your family warm while building an empire to keep them from going hungry in life.

ACKNOWLEDGMENTS

Thank you, God, for grace, mercy, compassion, and protection. My heart is full of gratitude to you for protecting us in the shelter and for protecting us in the penthouse. I belong to you God. I understand my purpose and am committed to my assignment on this earth. Speak through me in a way that is easily comprehensible and truly applicable. Have your way in my life. I will honor all the days of my life.

I would like to thank my two heartbeats for standing with me as I walked across the stage for the first time to accept my degree since their birth as my sincere supporters while holding my grandchildren nearby. You are all a reminder that everything I do has a greater meaning and exponential impact. I love you all.

Also, I would like to thank my extended family, including the mothers of my grandchildren, for being my family. Everyone needs someone to call family and I am proud and grateful for you to be mine.

Thank you to my pastor, Bishop T.D. Jakes, for being the vessel the Lord used to help me evolve spiritually, personally, and professionally.

Thank you to every person that purchased this book, read this love letter designed with your success in mind, and who finds ways to implement the strategies and concepts for maximum impact on the world around you.

I value and appreciate you!

IMPORTANT NOTE

The material in this book is for informational purposes only. It is not a contract in any form, nor is it a step-by-step guide. It is not intended to be more than an opportunity to share words of wisdom, share encouragement, spread firsthand experiences, and offer a glimmer of light to inspire that which was born in you to come to the surface.

This book is merely a tool to elevate your life and the actions and thoughts you have after reading it is your responsibility and reward.

The formatting of the book is intentional to encourage you to take notes as you read. Write encouraging messages to yourself as you work through the chapters and develop action steps with deadlines for yourself.

You are a courageous leader! You are a courageous leader! You are a courageous leader! Now go and do the work of the courageous leaders.

PRAYER

Almighty God,

I come before You today with my heart full of gratitude and hope. You are exalted above and beyond all else. Today I lift all the courageous leaders, especially those who are single parents, as they embark on the transformative journey of entrepreneurship. Alpha and Omega acknowledge the immense strength, resilience, and determination they have shown in balancing the demands of parenthood and the challenges of building a business.

God, you are asked for Your guidance and wisdom as they navigate this new path. Grant them clarity of vision, that they may see the opportunities that lie ahead and pursue them with unwavering faith. Help them to define their purpose and align their endeavors with their values, always striving for excellence and integrity in all they do.

As these leaders integrate artificial intelligence into their business ventures, we pray for open minds and receptive hearts. Remove any fear or apprehension about the future and the unknown. Fill them with confidence and courage to embrace the transformative power of AI. May they see it as a tool that enhances their capabilities, drives innovation, and creates new possibilities for growth and success.

Lord, bless their efforts with creativity and insight. Help them to leverage AI to make informed decisions, streamline operations, and deliver exceptional value to their customers. Guide them to use technology ethically and responsibly, ensuring that their businesses contribute positively to society and reflect Your love and compassion.

Surround these leaders with a dedicated and trustworthy support network. Bring mentors, advisors, and partners into their lives who will uplift, encourage, and guide them. Strengthen their connections with their families and communities, that they may find balance and joy in both their personal and professional lives.

Grant them resilience to overcome challenges, perseverance to pursue their goals, and the wisdom to learn from each experience. Help them to trust in Your plan and timing, knowing that You are with them every step of the way.

We pray for their well-being, Lord. Protect their health, nurture their mind, and sustain their spirit. May they find peace and fulfillment in their journey, and may their successes inspire and uplift others.

In Your infinite love and grace, we place these courageous leaders in Your hands. May they walk forward without fear, embracing the future with confidence, and integrating AI into their businesses as a testament to their faith in Your guidance and provision. To God be the glory forevermore.

Ase and Amen.

SECTION 1

CHAPTER 1: THE VISION

In entrepreneurship, especially as a single parent, your vision is the guiding light that steers your business towards success. A clear, compelling vision not only defines the purpose and direction of your business but also inspires and motivates you and your team to overcome challenges and achieve greatness. In this chapter, we will explore the importance of having a strong vision, the steps to define it, and share personal anecdotes and motivational stories to illustrate the transformative power of a well-defined vision.

A vision is more than just a dream or an idea; it is a concrete picture of what you want to achieve and the impact you wish to make. Here are key reasons why having a clear, compelling vision is crucial. A well-defined vision acts as a roadmap, guiding your decisions and actions. It helps you stay focused on your goals and avoid distractions that can derail your progress. A compelling vision energizes you and your team. It provides a sense of purpose and meaning, driving motivation and commitment even during challenging times.

Investors, partners, and customers are drawn to businesses with a sharp vision. It demonstrates your commitment and potential, making it easier to garner support and resources. Your vision sets the foundation for strategic planning. It helps you identify opportunities, set priorities, and allocate resources effectively to achieve your long-term goals. A strong vision encourages creative thinking and innovation. It inspires you to explore innovative ideas, take calculated risks, and continuously improve your products and services.

Write out your current vision statement below:

_____

_____

_____

Defining your vision is a deliberate and reflective process. Here are steps to help you articulate a clear and compelling vision for your business. Start by reflecting on your core values and passions. What drives you? What do you care deeply about? Your vision should align with your personal values and passions, as this will ensure authenticity and sustained motivation. Consider your strengths and what sets you apart from others. What unique skills, experiences, or perspectives do you bring to the table? Understanding your unique selling points will help you craft a vision that leverages your strengths. Conduct market research to understand the needs and desires of your target customers. What problems are they facing? How can your business address these issues? A vision that resonates with your customers' needs will be more compelling and impactful.

Be ready to articulate your long-term goals and aspirations. Where do you see your business in five or ten years? What milestones do you want to achieve? Setting specific, measurable, achievable, relevant, and time-bound (SMART) goals will provide clarity and direction. Write a concise and inspiring vision statement that encapsulates your aspirations. It should be clear, memorable, and motivating. Your vision statement should communicate what you aim to achieve and the impact you want to create. Share your vision statement with trusted advisors, mentors, your child(ren), and team members. Seek their feedback and be open to refining your vision based on their insights. A collaborative approach ensures that your vision resonates with others and is achievable.

To illustrate the power of vision, let's investigate some personal stories from single parent entrepreneurs who have defined their visions and achieved remarkable success. Sarah Thompson, a single mother of two, always had a passion for healthy living and wellness. After facing several health challenges, she realized the importance of holistic health practices. She envisioned creating a business that would provide affordable and accessible wellness products and services to busy parents like herself.

Sarah started by reflecting on her values of health, family, and community. She identified her unique strength as a certified nutritionist and wellness coach. Through market research, she discovered a gap in the market for affordable wellness solutions tailored to single parents. Sarah set long-term goals to create a wellness brand that would offer products, coaching, and community support. She crafted a vision statement: "To empower single parents to lead healthy, balanced lives through accessible and affordable wellness solutions."

With this vision, Sarah launched "Wellness for All," a company that offers a range of wellness products, online coaching, and a supportive community for single parents. Her clear and compelling vision attracted investors and customers who resonated with her mission. Today, Wellness for All has grown into a thriving business, helping thousands of single parents improve their health and well-being.

Michael Rodriguez, a single father, had a vision of creating a tech startup that would revolutionize online education for children. As a software engineer and a father, he understood the challenges of finding quality educational resources that engaged his children. Michael reflected on his values of education, innovation, and family. He identified his strength in technology and his passion for creating impactful solutions. Through extensive research, he realized the potential of AI in personalized learning and identified a need for engaging, adaptive educational platforms.

Michael set a long-term goal to develop an AI-powered educational platform that would make learning fun and effective for children. He crafted a vision statement: "To transform online education by creating personalized, engaging, and adaptive learning experiences for children worldwide. With a sharp vision, Michael founded "EduTech Kids," an AI-driven educational platform. His vision attracted talented developers and educators who shared his passion. The platform quickly gained traction, receiving positive feedback from parents and educators. EduTech Kids has since become a leading player in online education, helping millions of children enhance their learning experience.

The power of vision is undeniable. It provides direction, inspiration, and motivation, driving you and your business towards success. Your vision is the foundation upon which you build your dreams and aspirations. Reflect on your values, passions, and strengths. Understand your market and set long-term goals. Craft a clear and compelling vision statement and seek feedback to refine it. Your vision will not only guide your business but also attract resources, inspire your team, and foster innovation and growth.

Remember the stories of Sarah and Michael. Their journeys demonstrate how an unobstructed vision can transform challenges into opportunities and dreams into reality. Embrace your vision, stay committed to it, and let it guide you towards a future filled with success and fulfillment. Your vision is your most powerful tool. It will light your path, inspire those around you, and lead you to achieve greatness. Believe in your vision, protect it, and let it be the driving force that propels you and your business to new heights.

Now for just a moment drift into the space where you are prepped after reading this introduction and ready to deliver your elevator pitch to a room of eager investors. Write out the revised vision statement you would confidently deliver to a room filled with people that not only have immediate access to capital, but are eagerly ready to transfer funds to your commercial account today:

_____

_____

_____

_____

Now memorize your vision statement like it's your social security number and affirm it daily!

CHAPTER 2: THE COMMITMENT

Your vision should be the driving force behind your business. It is the spark that ignites your passion, the blueprint that guides your decisions, and the beacon that keeps you moving forward during challenging times. Staying true to your vision is crucial for achieving long-term success, yet it can be difficult to maintain focus amidst the complexities of balancing parenthood and entrepreneurship. This chapter delves into the challenges you may face, offers strategies to stay focused, and provides an inspiring case study of a single parent who stayed true to their vision despite significant obstacles.

As an entrepreneur your vision will be challenged, and for single parents, the challenges can be even more daunting. Here are some familiar challenges that may threaten your vision. Juggling the demands of parenthood and running a business often leaves little time for strategic planning and vision refinement. The day-to-day tasks can become overwhelming, making it difficult to focus on long-term goals. Financial stability is a major concern for single parent entrepreneurs. Limited resources and the constant need to secure funding can divert attention from your core vision to immediate survival. Dual responsibilities can lead to feelings of isolation.

Without a dedicated support network, it's easy to feel overwhelmed and disconnected from your entrepreneurial community. The pressure of raising children alone while trying to build a business can lead to self-doubt. Questioning your abilities and decisions can cloud your vision and undermine your confidence. Advice and opinions from well-meaning friends, family, and advisors can sometimes conflict with your vision. Balancing external feedback with your inner compass is a delicate act.

Despite these challenges, many single parent entrepreneurs successfully stay true to their vision. Here are some strategies to help you maintain focus and they will be repeated throughout this book due in part to their importance. Write down your vision statement. Clearly articulate what you want to achieve and why it matters. This will serve as a constant reminder and a guiding star during tough times. Break down your vision into Specific, Measurable, Achievable, Relevant, and Time-bound goals. This makes your vision more manageable and provides clear milestones to work towards. Visual representation of your vision can be incredibly powerful. Create a vision board with images, quotes, and symbols that reflect your goals. Place it where you can see it daily to keep your vision front and center.

An often-overlooked step is to outline the steps needed to achieve your vision. This includes marketing strategies, financial plans, and timelines. Regularly review and adjust your plan to stay aligned with your vision. Focus on high-impact activities that directly contribute to your vision. Learn to say no to tasks that do not align with your long-term goals. Use tools like to-do lists and time-blocking to manage your time effectively. I cannot emphasize enough how important it is to develop a support network so I will say it repeatedly, even if you get tired of seeing it notated throughout this book. I'm emphasizing it because I personally know how hard it is to work in isolation and push a vision forward. Surround yourself with supportive people who believe in your vision. Join entrepreneurial groups, seek mentors, and connect with other single parent entrepreneurs. A strong network can provide encouragement, advice, and practical assistance.

Taking care of your physical and mental well-being is essential. Regular exercise, healthy eating, and sufficient rest can boost your energy levels and mental clarity. Mindfulness practices such as meditation can help reduce stress and enhance focus. Flexibility is your friend. While it's important to stay true to your vision, flexibility is key. Be open to feedback and willing to pivot when necessary. Adaptability ensures that your vision evolves with changing circumstances without losing its core. Recognize and celebrate your progress. Small victories can provide motivation and reinforce your commitment to your vision. Rewarding yourself for achievements, no matter how small, can boost morale and maintain momentum.

Case Study: Jane's Journey to Success

Jane Thompson, a single mother of two, had a sharp vision: to create a sustainable fashion brand that empowers women and promotes environmental responsibility. Despite facing numerous challenges, Jane remained steadfast in her vision and achieved remarkable success.

Jane's journey began with limited financial resources. Balancing her time between raising her children and working a part-time job to support her family left her exhausted. The initial phase of her business involved long nights and weekends dedicated to designing and creating her clothing line.

In addition to financial and time constraints, Jane faced skepticism from friends and family who questioned the viability of her vision. She also struggled with self-doubt, wondering if she could successfully manage both her family and her business.

Stop for a second and reflect on what takes you off focus and causes you to deviate from your vision. Write out what it is so you can see it, know it, and drain it of it's energetic hold on you:

_____

_____

Strategies for Staying Focused

Jane wrote down her vision statement and posted it on her refrigerator. This daily reminder kept her motivated and focused on her long-term goals. Jane set specific goals for her business, such as launching her first collection within six months and reaching a certain number of sales by the end of the year. These goals provided direction and measurable milestones. Jane created a vision board filled with images of sustainable fashion, empowering quotes, and role models. This visual tool served as a source of inspiration and a constant reminder of her purpose.

Jane outlined a strategic plan that included market research, branding strategies, and financial projections. She regularly reviewed and adjusted her plan to stay on track. Jane focused on tasks that directly contributed to her vision, such as sourcing sustainable materials and building an online presence. She delegated household chores to her children, teaching them responsibility while freeing up her time. Here it comes again. Build a support network. Jane joined a local entrepreneurs' group and connected with mentors who provided valuable advice and support. She also found encouragement and practical tips from online communities of single parent entrepreneurs.

Jane made self-care a priority. She scheduled regular exercise, maintained a healthy diet, and practiced mindfulness meditation. These habits helped her manage stress and stay focused. When faced with challenges, Jane remained flexible. She adapted her designs based on customer feedback and explored fresh marketing channels to reach a wider audience. Jane celebrated every milestone, from her first sale to positive customer reviews. These small victories kept her motivated and reinforced her commitment to her vision.

Through perseverance and strategic focus, Jane successfully launched her sustainable fashion brand. Her business gained recognition for its unique designs and commitment to environmental responsibility. Jane's story was featured in several media outlets, inspiring other single parent entrepreneurs to pursue their visions.

Staying true to your vision as a single parent entrepreneur is undoubtedly challenging, but it is also immensely rewarding. By defining your vision clearly, setting SMART goals, prioritizing tasks, building a support network, and practicing self-care, you can overcome obstacles and stay focused on your path.

Jane's journey serves as a powerful reminder that with determination, strategic planning, and the right support, it is possible to achieve your vision despite the challenges. Embrace your journey, celebrate your progress, and remain steadfast in your commitment to your vision. Your unique perspective and resilience as a single parent entrepreneur is your greatest assets. Let them guide you towards achieving your dreams and making a lasting impact in your industry.

CHAPTER 3: THE OPPORTUNITY

Your vision should be the emotionless driving force behind your business. While economics and your heart are also important drivers, your vision is key. Your feelings will reach highs and lows all the time. Your vision must be void of emotions because during the fluctuations you have to stay on task. What you see as the solution to benefit some facet of the market is important to the health and direction of your business. It defines your goals, shapes your strategies, and inspires your actions. In the rapidly evolving metaverse, artificial intelligence (AI) presents unprecedented opportunities to align and enhance your vision. Embracing AI can help you streamline operations, make data-driven decisions, and innovate continuously. This chapter explores how AI can support your entrepreneurial vision, offering practical applications and expert insights into future trends.

AI is transforming the way businesses operate, making it possible to achieve goals more efficiently and effectively. By leveraging AI, you can align your entrepreneurial vision with innovative technology to drive growth and innovation. Here's how AI can enhance your vision. AI enables you to make informed decisions by analyzing large volumes of data. This data-driven approach helps you understand market trends, customer behavior, and operational efficiency, ensuring that your decisions are based on solid evidence rather than intuition alone. AI allows for the creation of personalized customer experiences. By analyzing customer data, AI can tailor marketing strategies, product recommendations, and customer service interactions to meet individual preferences, enhancing customer satisfaction and loyalty. AI automates routine tasks, reducing manual labor and minimizing errors. This increased efficiency allows you to focus on strategic activities that drive your vision forward, such as product development and market expansion. AI fosters innovation by providing insights that can lead to new products, services, and business models. By staying ahead of technological trends, you can maintain a competitive edge and continuously evolve your business.

AI offers numerous practical applications that can help you realize your entrepreneurial vision. Here are some key areas where AI can make a significant impact: AI can analyze customer data to provide deep insights into customer preferences, behaviors, and purchasing patterns. This information can be used to develop targeted marketing campaigns that resonate with your audience. For example, AI-powered tools can segment your customer base, identify high-value customers, and predict future buying behavior.

Case Study: AI-Driven Marketing at Sephora

Sephora, a global beauty retailer, uses AI to personalize customer experiences. The company's AI-powered chatbot, Sephora Virtual Artist, provides personalized product recommendations based on customers' preferences and previous purchases. This level of personalization has significantly increased customer engagement and sales.

AI can automate repetitive tasks, freeing up time and resources for more strategic activities. This includes tasks such as data entry, inventory management, and customer service. By automating these processes, you can improve efficiency, reduce costs, and enhance overall productivity.

Case Study: Automating Operations at XPO Logistics

XPO Logistics, a leading global planning company, uses AI to automate its supply chain operations. AI-powered robots manage tasks such as sorting, packing, and shipping, reducing operational costs and improving efficiency. This automation has allowed XPO Logistics to scale its operations and better serve its customers.

AI-powered predictive analytics can help you anticipate future trends and make initiative-taking decisions. By analyzing historical data and identifying patterns, AI can forecast sales, inventory needs, and market demand. This foresight enables you to plan more effectively and stay ahead of the competition.

Case Study: Predictive Analytics at Netflix

Netflix uses AI-driven predictive analytics to recommend content to its users. By analyzing viewing history and preferences, AI algorithms predict what users are likely to watch next, increasing viewer satisfaction and retention. This personalized approach has been a key factor in Netflix's success. AI can drive innovation by providing insights that lead to the development of new products and services. Machine learning algorithms can identify emerging trends and customer needs, enabling you to create offerings that meet market demand. Additionally, AI can optimize the product development process, reducing time to market.

Case Study: AI in Product Development at Procter & Gamble

Procter & Gamble (P&G) uses AI to innovate its product development process. By analyzing consumer data and market trends, AI identifies opportunities for new products and improvements to existing ones. This data-driven approach has resulted in successful product launches and increased market share for P&G.

To stay ahead in the age of AI, it's crucial to understand emerging trends and how they can impact your business. Here are some expert insights into the future of AI in entrepreneurship: Experts predict that AI will continue to revolutionize customer experience. As AI technology advances, businesses will be able to deliver even more personalized and seamless interactions. AI-powered virtual assistants and chatbots will become more sophisticated, providing instant, accurate, and empathetic responses to customer inquiries.

Quick, off the top of your head what products or services could you provide or improve with the incremental addition of AI implementation?

_____

_____

According to Gartner, by 2025, AI-driven technologies will oversee 95% of customer interactions. This shift will enhance customer satisfaction and reduce the need for human intervention in routine tasks, allowing businesses to focus on complex issues that require a distinctive touch. As AI becomes more integrated into business operations, ethical considerations will take center stage. Businesses will need to ensure that their AI systems are transparent, fair, and accountable. This includes addressing issues such as data privacy, algorithmic bias, and the ethical use of AI in decision-making processes.

IBM emphasizes the importance of ethical AI, advocating for guidelines and best practices to ensure responsible AI development. By prioritizing ethical considerations, businesses can build trust with their customers and stakeholders, fostering long-term success.

AI will continue to transform the workforce, augmenting human capabilities and creating new opportunities. Rather than replacing jobs, AI will enhance them, allowing employees to focus on higher-value tasks that require creativity, critical thinking, and emotional intelligence. My peer, McKinsey & Company, predicts that by 2030, AI will create more jobs than it displaces, particularly in fields such as healthcare, education, and creative industries. This shift will require businesses to invest in reskilling and upskilling their workforce to adapt to the changing job arena.

As a single parent entrepreneur, your vision is your greatest asset. In the age of AI, aligning your vision with advanced technology can propel your business to new heights. By leveraging AI, you can make data-driven decisions, personalize customer experiences, automate processes, and drive innovation. The practical applications and expert insights discussed in this chapter provide a roadmap for integrating AI into your business strategy. Embrace AI not as a replacement for human ingenuity but as a powerful tool that enhances your capabilities and supports your vision. By staying informed about future trends and prioritizing ethical considerations, you can build a sustainable, competitive, and forward-thinking business.

The road ahead of you as a single parent entrepreneur is a testament to your level of resilience and determination. With AI as your ally, the possibilities for realizing your vision are limitless. Step into the future with confidence, harness the power of AI, and continue to redefine what's possible in the world of entrepreneurship. Your vision, empowered by technology, can change not only your business but also the lives of those you touch.

What fear do you have about AI?

_____

_____

What opportunity do you see with the use of AI?

_____

_____

What do you think could change for you by using AI?

_____

_____

If you are already using AI, how can you elevate your use?

_____

_____

_____

SECTION 2

CHAPTER 4: THE EMBRACE

In the ever-evolving universe of business, technology has emerged as a crucial ally for entrepreneurs. For single parents juggling the demands of parenthood and entrepreneurship, leveraging artificial intelligence (AI) can be a notable change. This chapter delves into understanding AI, its potential benefits, and practical ways single parent entrepreneurs can harness its power to transform their businesses. We will also explore an inspiring case study of a business that successfully integrated AI to achieve remarkable growth and efficiency.

Artificial Intelligence (AI) refers to the simulation of human intelligence in machines that are programmed to think, learn, and adapt. These intelligent systems can perform tasks that typically require human intelligence, such as visual perception, speech recognition, decision-making, and language translation. AI technologies include machine learning, natural language processing, robotics, and computer vision, among others.

The potential benefits of AI for businesses are vast and transformative. AI algorithms analyze large volumes of data to provide actionable insights, enabling businesses to make informed decisions. This leads to more accurate forecasting, better risk management, and improved strategic planning. Automation of routine tasks through AI reduces operational costs and increases productivity. For instance, AI can streamline processes such as inventory management, customer service, and marketing, allowing entrepreneurs to focus on more strategic activities. AI enhances customer interactions by providing personalized experiences. Through machine learning algorithms, businesses can analyze customer behavior and preferences to deliver tailored recommendations, improving customer satisfaction and loyalty.

AI drives innovation by enabling the development of new products and services. It opens opportunities for businesses to explore new markets, enhance existing offerings, and stay competitive in a rapidly changing landscape. As a single parent entrepreneur, integrating AI into your business strategy can provide a significant advantage. Here are practical ways to leverage AI effectively.

Use AI-powered tools to automate repetitive tasks, such as scheduling appointments, managing emails, and processing invoices. This saves time and allows you to focus on high-value activities that require your expertise and creativity. Implement AI-driven chatbots and virtual assistants to manage customer inquiries and support. These tools provide quick and accurate responses, improving customer satisfaction and freeing up your time to address more complex issues. Utilize AI to analyze customer data and behavior, enabling you to create targeted marketing campaigns. AI can help identify trends, segment your audience, and personalize marketing messages, leading to higher engagement and conversion rates.

Leverage AI-powered financial tools to manage budgeting, forecasting, and expense tracking. These tools provide real-time insights into your financial health, helping you make informed decisions and maintain financial stability. AI can optimize your supply chain by predicting demand, managing inventory, and improving planning. This ensures that you have the right products available at the right time, reducing costs and enhancing efficiency. AI-driven platforms offer personalized learning experiences, allowing you to acquire new skills and knowledge at your own pace. This is particularly beneficial for staying updated with industry trends and advancements.

Case Study: A Business Transformed by AI

Emma Roberts, a single mother of two, founded Bright Horizons Learning Center, an early childhood education center, with a mission to provide high-quality, affordable childcare and education. Despite her passion and dedication, Emma faced numerous challenges in managing the day-to-day operations and ensuring the sustainability of her business.

Emma struggled with administrative tasks, staff scheduling, and providing personalized learning experiences for the children. These challenges consumed a significant amount of her time, leaving her overwhelmed and unable to focus on strategic growth.

Recognizing the potential of AI, Emma decided to integrate AI-powered solutions into her business. She implemented the following technologies. Emma introduced an AI-based administrative platform that automated scheduling, attendance tracking, and billing. This tool reduced the time spent on paperwork and minimized errors, allowing Emma to focus on enhancing the center's educational programs. To provide personalized learning experiences, Emma adopted an AI-powered educational platform that assessed each child's learning style, strengths, and areas for improvement. The platform generated customized lesson plans and activities, ensuring that each child received the support they needed to thrive. Emma implemented an AI-driven communication system that kept parents informed about their child's progress, upcoming events, and important announcements. The system used natural language processing to understand and respond to parents' inquiries, providing timely and accurate information. Using AI-based scheduling software, Emma optimized staff shifts based on demand and availability. This ensured that the center was always adequately staffed, improving efficiency and employee satisfaction.

The integration of AI transformed Bright Horizons Learning Center in several ways. Administrative tasks were streamlined, reducing Emma's workload, and allowing her to focus on strategic initiatives. The automated scheduling system ensured smooth operations and minimized conflicts. The personalized learning platform led to significant improvements in children's academic performance and engagement. Parents reported higher satisfaction with the individualized attention their children received.

The AI-driven communication system fostered better relationships between the center and parents. Timely updates and personalized responses increased parental trust and involvement in their child's education. The optimized scheduling system improved staff morale and reduced turnover. Employees appreciated the fair and efficient allocation of shifts, leading to a more positive work environment. With more time to focus on strategic planning, Emma expanded the center's services and opened a second location. The use of AI also attracted new families seeking innovative educational solutions for their children.

Emma's story illustrates the transformative power of AI in overcoming challenges and achieving business growth. By embracing AI, she not only improved the efficiency and quality of her services but also created a sustainable and scalable business model.

Artificial Intelligence is a powerful tool that can revolutionize the way single parent entrepreneurs run their businesses. By automating routine tasks, enhancing customer experiences, optimizing operations, and driving innovation, AI provides a significant competitive edge. The case study of Bright Horizons Learning Center demonstrates how AI can transform challenges into opportunities, leading to remarkable growth and success.

As a single parent entrepreneur, embracing AI and technology is not just a strategic move; it is a necessity in today's rapidly evolving world. By leveraging AI, you can achieve greater efficiency, scalability, and sustainability, all while balancing the demands of parenthood and entrepreneurship. The future is bright for those who dare to innovate and lead with the power of artificial intelligence.

Remember, the journey of integrating AI into your business is continuous and ever evolving. Stay curious, keep learning, and be open to new possibilities. With determination, resilience, and the right technological tools, you can overcome any challenge and redefine what it means to be a successful single parent entrepreneur.

CHAPTER 5: THE IMPLEMENTATION

I'm certain your days are constantly marked by resilience, multitasking, and the ability to navigate complex challenges as a single parent. These qualities make you well-suited to leverage the transformative power of artificial intelligence (AI) in your business. Integrating AI can streamline operations, enhance customer experiences, and drive innovation. This chapter provides practical steps for implementing AI tools, highlights real-world applications, and shares inspiring success stories to guide and motivate you on this path as a founder and business owner. Implementing AI in your business might seem daunting, but with a structured approach, it can become a manageable and rewarding endeavor. Here are practical steps to guide you through the process:

Begin by identifying areas in your business where AI can add the most value. This could be in customer service, marketing, operations, or product development. (1) Conduct a thorough analysis of your business processes to pinpoint inefficiencies and opportunities for improvement. (2) Establish clear objectives for your AI implementation. (3) Determine what you want to achieve, whether it's improving customer satisfaction, increasing operational efficiency, or driving sales. Having specific goals will help you measure the success of your AI initiatives. Gain a basic understanding of AI and its capabilities. There are numerous online resources, courses, and webinars available that can provide foundational knowledge. Ensure your team is also educated about AI and its potential benefits.

Now is the time to select AI tools that align with your business needs and objectives. Start with simple, ready-to-use AI applications before moving on to more complex solutions. Popular AI tools for small businesses include chatbots (e.g., Drift, Tidio), customer relationship management (CRM) systems (e.g., Salesforce, HubSpot), and marketing automation platforms (e.g., Mailchimp, Marketo).

Start small by implementing AI in small, manageable pilot projects. This allows you to evaluate the effectiveness of AI tools on a smaller scale before committing to a full-scale rollout. Use pilot projects to gather data, measure impact, and refine your approach. Continuously monitor and evaluate the performance of AI tools. Use key performance indicators (KPIs) to measure success against your objectives.

Analyze the results to understand what's working and what needs improvement. Once you've validated the success of your pilot projects, scale up the implementation of AI tools across your business. Ensure you have the necessary infrastructure and resources to support larger-scale AI applications. Encourage a culture that embraces innovation and continuous improvement. Involve your team in AI initiatives and create an environment where experimentation and learning are valued.

AI can revolutionize various aspects of your business. It can be used in customer service. AI-powered chatbots and virtual assistants can manage routine customer inquiries, provide instant responses, and offer personalized assistance. This enhances customer satisfaction and frees up your team to focus on more complex issues.

For example, Tidio offers a chatbot platform that integrates with your website and social media channels to provide seamless customer support. AI-powered financial tools can automate bookkeeping, generate financial reports, and provide insights into cash flow and expenses. QuickBooks, for example, uses AI to categorize transactions, detect anomalies, and offer financial forecasts.

Have you thought about using AI for marketing and sales? AI can optimize your marketing efforts through predictive analytics, personalized content, and automated campaigns. Tools like HubSpot use AI to analyze customer behavior, segment audiences, and deliver targeted marketing messages. This increases engagement and drives conversions.

AI can streamline inventory management by predicting demand, optimizing stock levels, and reducing waste. For instance, Clear AI offers solutions that use machine learning algorithms to forecast inventory needs and automate replenishment processes. AI can accelerate product development by analyzing market trends, identifying customer needs, and predicting product performance. Tools like IBM Watson offer AI-powered analytics that can guide product design and innovation.

Case Study: Single Parent Entrepreneur Transforms Business with AI

Meet Jane Doe, a single parent who founded a small online retail business selling handmade jewelry. Balancing her responsibilities as a parent and entrepreneur was challenging, and she struggled with managing customer inquiries, marketing, and inventory. Jane realized that to scale her business, she needed to streamline operations and enhance customer experiences. She decided to explore AI solutions that could address these challenges.

Jane implemented Tidio, an AI-powered chatbot, on her website. The chatbot managed routine customer inquiries, provided product recommendations, and assisted with order tracking. This not only improved customer satisfaction but also freed up Jane's time to focus on strategic tasks. To boost her marketing efforts, Jane adopted HubSpot's AI-driven marketing platform. The tool analyzed customer behavior, segmented her audience, and delivered personalized email campaigns. This led to higher engagement rates and increased sales. Jane integrated Clear AI's inventory management solution. The AI tool predicted demand patterns, optimized stock levels, and automated replenishment orders. This reduced stockouts and overstock situations, improving her cash flow.

Within six months of implementing AI tools, Jane saw remarkable improvements in her business. The AI chatbot reduced response times and provided 24/7 support, leading to a 30% increase in customer satisfaction scores. Personalized marketing campaigns driven by AI resulted in a 25% increase in sales and a significant boost in customer loyalty. AI-powered inventory management reduced excess inventory by 20% and improved cash flow, allowing Jane to reinvest in her business.

According to Jane, "Integrating AI into my business was a meaningful change. It allowed me to manage my time more effectively, improve customer experiences, and scale my business. As a single parent, it's empowering to see how technology can help achieve a better work-life balance while driving business growth."

Sarah, a single mother running a local boutique, struggled with attracting and retaining customers. She implemented an AI-powered CRM system to track customer preferences and send personalized offers. This led to a 40% increase in repeat customers and boosted her sales significantly. Sarah now uses AI to forecast trends and stock her boutique with items her customers love.

John, a single father with a tech startup, faced challenges in providing timely customer support. He integrated an AI chatbot into his support system, which handled basic inquiries and troubleshooting. This improved response times and customer satisfaction. John's business grew as he could focus on product development while the AI chatbot managed customer support effectively.

Lisa, a single parent, and freelance graphic designer found managing her finances overwhelming. She adopted QuickBooks' AI-powered financial tools to automate invoicing, expense tracking, and financial reporting. This not only saved her time but also provided insights into her business's financial health, helping her make informed decisions and grow her freelance practice.

As a single parent entrepreneur, integrating AI into your business can be a transformative journey. By following practical steps, leveraging real-world applications, and drawing inspiration from success stories, you can harness the power of AI to streamline operations, enhance customer experiences, and drive growth. Remember, the key to success lies in starting small, continuously learning, and fostering a culture of innovation. Embrace AI as a valuable ally in your entrepreneurial journey and witness the remarkable impact it can have on your business and life.

By implementing AI, you are not only positioning your business for success but also setting a powerful example for your children and community. Your journey as a single parent entrepreneur, empowered by AI, is a testament to the incredible possibilities that arise when resilience meets innovation. Keep pushing forward, stay curious, and let AI be the catalyst that propels your business to new heights.

Can you list 3 specific AI tools you can add or upgrade for process improvements and if so, what are they?

_____

_____

_____

Can you list 3 specific AI tools you can add or upgrade for system improvements and if so, what are they?

_____

_____

_____

CHAPTER 6: THE ADVANCEMENTS

In today's rapidly evolving business landscape, staying ahead of technological changes is not just advantageous—it's essential. For single parent entrepreneurs, this challenge may seem even more daunting due to the balancing act of managing family and business. However, by embracing continuous learning and adaptation, you can turn technological advancements into powerful tools that drive success and innovation. This chapter provides practical insights on keeping up with technology and shares an inspiring case study of an entrepreneur who thrived by staying ahead of the curve.

Technological advancements are reshaping every industry, creating new opportunities, and disrupting traditional business models. For entrepreneurs, particularly single parents juggling multiple responsibilities, keeping pace with these changes is crucial for several reasons. Staying current with technology helps you maintain a competitive edge. By leveraging the latest tools and innovations, you can streamline operations, enhance customer experiences, and stay ahead of competitors.

Technology can significantly boost efficiency and productivity. Automation tools, for example, can handle repetitive tasks, freeing up your time to focus on strategic initiatives and family responsibilities. Today's customers are tech-savvy and expect seamless, tech-driven interactions. By adopting the latest technologies, you can meet and exceed customer expectations, fostering loyalty and satisfaction.

Embracing innovative technologies can spur innovation and open new revenue streams. Whether it's developing new products or entering new markets, technology can be a catalyst for growth and expansion. Keeping up with technological advancements requires a proactive approach. Here are some effective strategies to stay informed and ahead of the curve. Platforms like Coursera, Udacity, and LinkedIn Learning offer a plethora of courses on the latest technologies. These courses allow you to learn at your own pace and gain practical skills that can be directly applied to your business.
Participate in webinars and workshops hosted by industry experts. These events provide valuable insights into emerging trends and best practices. Dedicate time to reading industry blogs, journals, and whitepapers. Websites like TechCrunch, Wired, and Harvard Business Review are excellent resources for staying updated on technological trends.

Be knowledgeable by joining professional associations. Becoming a member of professional associations related to your industry can provide access to exclusive resources, events, and a network of like-minded professionals. Conferences and trade shows offer opportunities to gain experience about the latest technologies and network with industry leaders. Participate in online forums and social media groups focused on technology and entrepreneurship. Platforms like Reddit, LinkedIn, and Slack have vibrant communities where you can exchange ideas and stay informed.

Consider partnering with technology consultants who can provide expert advice on implementing and optimizing modern technologies. Establish relationships with software vendors who can offer training, support, and updates on their products. Engage with innovation hubs and incubators that offer access to innovative technologies, mentorship, and funding opportunities. The ability to continuously learn and adapt is a hallmark of successful entrepreneurs. Here's how you can cultivate this mindset.

Embrace the belief that your abilities and knowledge can be developed through dedication and hard work. A growth mindset fosters a love for learning and resilience in the face of challenges. Establish specific, measurable learning goals to stay motivated and focused. For example, aim to complete a certain number of online courses or attend a set number of industry events each year. Encourage a culture of experimentation within your business. Assess innovative technologies on a small scale before full implementation. This approach allows you to learn from failures and successes without significant risk. Regularly reflect on your experiences and the outcomes of new initiatives. Use these reflections to make informed adjustments and continuously improve your strategies and processes.

Case Study: Thriving by Staying Ahead of the Curve

Meet Laura Johnson, a single mother and founder of TechSavvy Tutors, an innovative online tutoring platform that leverages AI to provide personalized learning experiences for students. Laura's journey is a testament to the power of staying ahead of technological changes. Laura always had a passion for education and technology. After a career in teaching and raising two children on her own, she identified a gap in the market for personalized, technology-driven tutoring services. She envisioned a platform that could adapt to each student's learning style and pace, providing tailored support and improving educational outcomes.

Laura's first step was to immerse herself in the latest advancements in educational technology and artificial intelligence. She enrolled in online courses on AI and machine learning, attended EdTech conferences, and joined professional associations such as the International Society for Technology in Education (ISTE). Armed with knowledge and a sharp vision, Laura collaborated with AI experts to develop an intelligent tutoring system. The platform uses AI algorithms to assess students' strengths and weaknesses, adapting lessons in real-time to meet their individual needs. She also integrated features like interactive video lessons, gamified learning modules, and real-time progress tracking.

The journey forward was not without challenges. As a single parent, Laura had to balance her entrepreneurial pursuits with parenting duties. She leveraged her network for support, seeking advice from mentors and forming partnerships with other EdTech startups. She also implemented efficient time management strategies, such as scheduling dedicated work hours and using productivity tools to stay organized. TechSavvy Tutors quickly gained traction, attracting thousands of students, and receiving positive feedback from parents and educators. The platform's innovative approach to personalized learning sets it apart from traditional tutoring services. Laura's commitment to continuous learning and adaptation enabled her to stay ahead of competitors and consistently improve the platform's offerings.

Today, TechSavvy Tutors is a leading online tutoring platform, helping students worldwide achieve academic success. Laura's story is an inspiring example of how embracing technology and staying ahead of the curve can lead to remarkable achievements. Her journey underscores the importance of continuous learning, resilience, and the willingness to adapt.

Staying ahead of technological changes is not a one-time effort but an ongoing journey. As a single parent entrepreneur, you have already demonstrated incredible resilience and adaptability. By embracing continuous learning and actively seeking out recent technologies, you can turn challenges into opportunities and drive your business towards sustainable success. Remember, you are not alone on this journey. Leverage your network, seek out resources, and remain open to innovative ideas and innovations. Your ability to stay ahead of technological advancements will not only enhance your business but also inspire others to do the same.

As you navigate the ever-evolving industry of technology, keep pushing forward with confidence and curiosity. The future holds endless possibilities for those who dare to innovate and lead with vision. Your unique path is a testament to the power of perseverance and the incredible potential of single parent entrepreneurs. Embrace the challenges, celebrate the victories, and continue to stay ahead of the curve. The world is waiting for your next big idea.

What new technology are you curious about?

_____

_____

_____

_____

SECTION 3

CHAPTER 7: THE LEGALITIES

Navigating legal and ethical challenges is crucial for sustainable success. For single parent entrepreneurs, balancing these aspects alongside personal responsibilities can seem daunting. This chapter aims to demystify the complexities surrounding intellectual property (IP) protection and ethical considerations in AI usage. Additionally, it presents a compelling case study that illustrates how to effectively manage legal challenges, providing both insight and inspiration.

Intellectual Property (IP) is a cornerstone of your business's value, encompassing creations of the mind such as inventions, literary and artistic works, designs, symbols, names, and images used in commerce. As a single parent entrepreneur, understanding and protecting your IP is essential to safeguarding your business's competitive edge. There are four distinct types of intellectual property that you should be aware of as you move through your seed stage to scaling your business:

1. Patents: Protects inventions and discoveries. A patent gives you the exclusive right to make, use, and sell your invention for a certain number of years. This is critical if your business is based on a unique product or process.

2. Trademarks: Protects brand names, logos, and slogans that distinguish your products or services. Trademarks prevent others from using similar marks that could confuse customers.

3. Copyrights: Protects original works of authorship, such as books, music, and software. Copyright gives you the exclusive right to use and distribute your work.

4. Trade Secrets: Protects confidential business information that provides a competitive edge, such as formulas, practices, and designs.

Conduct an audit to identify what IP assets your business holds. Ensure that patents, trademarks, and copyrights are registered with the appropriate government bodies. This provides legal protection and strengthens your position in case of infringement. Use non-disclosure agreements (NDAs) to protect trade secrets and sensitive information when dealing with employees, contractors, and partners. Regularly monitor the market for potential infringements and act when necessary. This could involve sending cease-and-desist letters or pursuing legal action.

Artificial Intelligence (AI) offers immense potential for innovation and efficiency, but it also raises important ethical questions. As a single parent entrepreneur, integrating AI responsibly is essential for building a business that is both successful and ethically sound. AI systems can inadvertently perpetuate biases present in their training data. It's crucial to ensure that your AI solutions are fair and unbiased. This involves using diverse and representative datasets, and regularly auditing AI systems for bias.

Customers and stakeholders should understand how AI is being used in your business. Transparency builds trust, while accountability ensures that there are mechanisms in place to address any issues that arise from AI usage. AI often requires substantial amounts of data, raising concerns about privacy and security. Implement robust data protection measures and ensure compliance with relevant regulations, such as GDPR. AI can automate tasks, potentially displacing workers. Consider how your AI implementation affects your workforce and explore ways to upskill employees for new roles created by AI technologies.

Create a set of ethical guidelines for AI usage in your business, outlining your commitment to fairness, transparency, and accountability. Engage with stakeholders, including customers and employees, to understand their concerns and expectations regarding AI. Regularly review and update your AI systems and practices to ensure they remain ethical and compliant with emerging standards and regulations. Invest in education and training for yourself and your team on the ethical implications of AI and how to address them.

Case Study: Navigating Legal Challenges Successfully

Meet Sarah, a single parent entrepreneur who founded a tech startup specializing in AI-driven educational tools. Her innovative platform used machine learning to personalize learning experiences for students, gaining significant traction in the edtech market. However, as her business grew, so did the legal challenges. Sarah's company faced two major legal challenges: an intellectual property dispute and concerns about the ethical use of AI.

A larger competitor accused Sarah's company of infringing on their patented technology, threatening legal action. Stakeholders raised concerns about potential biases in the AI algorithms, questioning the fairness and transparency of the platform. Sarah tackled these challenges methodically, drawing on both legal advice and her commitment to ethical business practices.

Sarah consulted with an IP attorney to review the claims and her company's patents. The attorney confirmed that her technology was original and non-infringing. Instead of escalating to a costly court battle, Sarah opted for mediation. She presented evidence of her independent development and proposed a licensing agreement to avoid future conflicts. The competitor agreed to a mutually beneficial licensing agreement, allowing Sarah's company to continue using the technology while paying a reasonable fee. This not only resolved the dispute but also established a potential partnership.

Sarah commissioned an independent audit of her AI algorithms to identify and address any biases. The audit revealed certain areas where improvements were needed. Her team revised the algorithms, incorporating more diverse datasets and implementing fairness measures to ensure equitable outcomes for all users. Sarah launched an initiative to increase transparency, including publishing detailed reports on how the AI system worked and its impact on different user groups. By addressing these concerns proactively, Sarah regained the trust of her stakeholders. Her commitment to ethical AI practices was recognized in industry publications, enhancing her company's reputation.

Early and proactive legal consultation can prevent disputes from escalating. Understanding your IP rights and seeking expert advice is crucial. Prioritizing ethical considerations in AI usage not only mitigates risks but also builds trust and credibility with stakeholders. Opting for mediation and negotiation can lead to more favorable and less adversarial outcomes than litigation. Being transparent about AI practices and actively addressing concerns can turn potential challenges into opportunities for positive recognition.

As a single parent entrepreneur, navigating legal and ethical considerations may seem overwhelming, but it is essential for building a sustainable and reputable business. Protecting your intellectual property ensures that your innovative ideas remain secure and profitable. Embracing ethical AI practices fosters trust and long-term success.

Sarah's case study illustrates that with the right approach, legal challenges can be managed effectively, and ethical concerns can be addressed proactively. By staying informed, seeking expert advice, and committing to ethical standards, you can navigate these complexities with confidence.

Your journey as an entrepreneur is marked by resilience and determination. Embrace these legal and ethical considerations not as hurdles, but as integral components of your path to success. With the right strategies and mindset, you can protect your vision, build a responsible business, and inspire others with your leadership.

Never forget, all the challenges you overcome not only strengthens your business but also set an example for your children and community. Your dedication to doing what is right, even in the face of adversity, will pave the way for a brighter future for both your business and those who look up to you.

CHAPTER 8: THE SUSTAINABILITY

Building a sustainable business is not just about ensuring long-term profitability; it's about creating a positive impact on society and the environment. For single parent entrepreneurs, the quest for sustainability is even more significant. It encompasses securing a stable future for their families while contributing to a healthier planet and a more equitable world. This chapter will delve into the core principles of long-term planning, environmental and social responsibility, and illustrate these concepts through a real-world case study.

Long-term planning is the foundation of a sustainable business. It involves setting clear, achievable goals, developing strategic initiatives, and continuously adapting to changes in the market and environment. Here are key steps to building a sustainable business through long-term planning. Define a sharp vision and mission that emphasizes sustainability. This provides direction and purpose, guiding your business decisions and actions. Set strategic goals that align with your vision and mission. These goals should encompass financial targets, environmental objectives, and social responsibilities. Ensure they are Specific, Measurable, Achievable, Relevant, and Time-bound (SMART).

Efficient resource management is crucial for sustainability. This includes optimizing the use of materials, energy, and human resources. Implement practices that reduce waste and enhance productivity. Foster a culture of innovation to stay ahead of market trends and technological advancements. Be adaptable to change, whether it's evolving customer preferences or new regulatory requirements. Develop a robust financial plan that ensures long-term stability. This involves budgeting, forecasting, and managing cash flow effectively. Consider diversifying revenue streams to mitigate risks.

Building a sustainable business goes beyond financial success; it involves taking responsibility for your environmental footprint and social impact. Here are strategies to integrate environmental and social responsibility into your business model. Adopt sustainable practices in your operations. This could include using renewable energy sources, reducing carbon emissions, implementing recycling programs, and minimizing water usage. Design and offer products that are environmentally friendly. Use sustainable materials, reduce packaging waste, and ensure your products are recyclable or biodegradable.

Engage with your local community to understand their needs and contribute positively. This could involve supporting local suppliers, participating in community projects, and providing employment opportunities. Ensure fair labor practices within your business. This includes providing fair wages, safe working conditions, and opportunities for employee growth and development. Source materials and products ethically. Partner with suppliers who share your commitment to sustainability and social responsibility.

Case Study: Patagonia - Balancing Profit with Purpose

Patagonia, an outdoor apparel company, is a stellar example of a business that balances profit with purpose. Founded by Yvon Chouinard in 1973, Patagonia has built a reputation for its commitment to environmental and social responsibility. Patagonia has implemented numerous initiatives to minimize its environmental impact. The company uses recycled materials in its products, such as polyester from plastic bottles and reclaimed cotton. In 1996, Patagonia made the groundbreaking decision to use only organic cotton in its clothing, despite the higher costs and sourcing challenges.

In addition to sustainable materials, Patagonia is committed to reducing waste. The company's "Worn Wear" program encourages customers to repair and reuse their clothing instead of buying the latest items. Patagonia also offers a lifetime guarantee on its products, promoting longevity over fast fashion. Patagonia's commitment to social responsibility is evident in its fair labor practices and community engagement. The company ensures that its workers, both in its facilities and its supply chain, are treated ethically and paid fairly. Patagonia is a founding member of the Fair Labor Association, which audits and ensures fair labor conditions across its supply chain.

Patagonia also donates 1% of its sales to environmental causes through its "1% for the Planet" initiative. Since its inception, Patagonia has contributed over $89 million to environmental nonprofits, supporting projects ranging from wildlife preservation to climate action. Patagonia's dedication to sustainability has not hindered its financial success. In fact, it has bolstered the company's reputation and customer loyalty. Consumers are increasingly seeking brands that align with their values, and Patagonia's transparent and ethical practices resonate strongly with this demographic.

The company's innovative approach to business has led to substantial growth. Patagonia reported over $1 billion in revenue in 2018, demonstrating that it is possible to achieve financial success while prioritizing sustainability and social responsibility.

For single parent entrepreneurs, integrating sustainability into your business may seem daunting. However, by taking incremental steps, you can build a business that thrives financially while contributing positively to society and the environment. Begin with small, manageable changes. Implementing recycling programs, reducing energy consumption, or switching to eco-friendly packaging are simple yet impactful steps.

Utilize technology to enhance sustainability. AI and data analytics can optimize resource management, improve supply chain efficiency, and reduce waste. Partner with other businesses and organizations that share your commitment to sustainability. Collaboration can lead to shared resources, knowledge, and greater impact. Continuously educate yourself and your team about sustainability practices and innovations. Attend workshops, webinars, and industry conferences to stay informed. Involve your customers in your sustainability journey. Educate them about your practices, encourage them to make eco-friendly choices, and solicit their feedback for improvement. Regularly measure your environmental and social impact. Reporting on your progress not only holds you accountable but also builds trust with stakeholders and customers.

Building a sustainable business will lead you down a path that requires dedication, innovation, and a commitment to ethical practices. For single parent entrepreneurs, this journey is especially meaningful as it aligns with the desire to create a better future for their families and communities. By focusing on long-term planning, embracing environmental and social responsibility, and drawing inspiration from successful examples like Patagonia, you can build a business that balances profit with purpose. Remember, sustainability is not just a trend; it's a necessity for the longevity and success of your business.

As you navigate this path, take pride in the positive impact you are making. Your efforts contribute to a healthier planet, a fairer society, and a brighter future for the next generation. Embrace the challenge, celebrate the successes, and continue to innovate. The journey of building a sustainable business is rewarding, inspiring, and transformative.

Sources
- "Patagonia's Anti-Growth Strategy" by The New Yorker.
- "The Cleanest Line: A Patagonia Story" by Vincent Stanley.

CHAPTER 9: THE CRISIS

Every entrepreneur, at some point, faces a crisis. For single parent entrepreneurs, the stakes are often higher, as they must navigate business challenges while ensuring their family's stability. Effective crisis management is not just about surviving; it's about leveraging tough times to emerge stronger and more resilient. This chapter will explore strategies for preparing for and managing crises, highlight the importance of resilience and adaptability, and share an inspiring case study of a single parent entrepreneur who turned a crisis into an opportunity.

The first step in effective crisis management is anticipating potential crises. This initiative-taking approach allows you to create contingency plans and minimize the impact of unforeseen events. Identify risks in your business environment, such as financial challenges, market fluctuations, natural disasters, and personal emergencies. Conduct a SWOT analysis (Strengths, Weaknesses, Opportunities, Threats) to understand vulnerabilities and prepare accordingly. Create a comprehensive crisis management plan that includes clear protocols for several types of crises. Define roles and responsibilities within your team, ensuring everyone knows their part during a crisis. Establish communication strategies to keep stakeholders informed and manage public relations.

Preparedness for AI is critical just as earthquake or storm preparedness. Build a financial cushion by maintaining an emergency fund that covers at least three to six months of operating expenses. Diversify revenue streams to reduce dependency on a lone source of income. Implement robust cybersecurity measures to protect your business data. Regularly back up critical data and ensure you have access to necessary tools and resources in case of a technology failure. When a crisis hits, how you respond can make all the difference.

Effective crisis management involves swift action, clear communication, and maintaining a calm demeanor. Assess the situation quickly to understand the scope and impact of the crisis. Activate your crisis management plan, mobilizing your team and resources as outlined. Communicate transparently with your team, customers, and stakeholders. Provide regular updates to keep everyone informed. Use multiple communication channels (email, social media, press releases) to reach your audience effectively.

Focus on finding solutions rather than dwelling on the problem. Engage your team in brainstorming and decision-making processes. Prioritize actions that mitigate the crisis's impact on your business and family. Address customer concerns promptly and empathetically. Offer solutions and support to maintain trust and loyalty. Consider offering discounts, refunds, or other compensations to affected customers. Keep detailed records of actions taken during the crisis. This documentation will be valuable for post-crisis analysis and future preparedness.

Resilience is the ability to bounce back from adversity. For single parent entrepreneurs, building resilience is crucial to navigating both personal and professional challenges. Cultivate a positive and growth-oriented mindset. Embrace challenges as opportunities for learning and growth. Practice mindfulness and stress management techniques to maintain mental and emotional well-being. Lean on your support network of family, friends, mentors, and fellow entrepreneurs. Their encouragement and advice can provide strength during tough times. Join entrepreneurial groups or online communities to share experiences and gain insights from others facing similar challenges.

Prioritize self-care to ensure you remain physically and mentally fit to manage crises. Regular exercise, adequate sleep, and healthy eating are essential. Set aside time for activities that rejuvenate you, such as hobbies, meditation, or spending time with loved ones. Invest in continuous learning and skill development to enhance your adaptability. Stay updated on industry trends and best practices. Attend workshops, webinars, and conferences to expand your knowledge and network.

Adaptability is the ability to adjust to new conditions. It's a vital skill for navigating the evolution of business today. Be open to revising your business plans and strategies in response to changing circumstances. Flexibility allows you to pivot and seize new opportunities. Encourage a culture of innovation within your team, where experimentation and creative problem-solving are valued.

Embrace technology to streamline operations and enhance efficiency. Tools like cloud computing, project management software, and AI can help manage tasks more effectively. Explore digital marketing strategies to reach new customers and expand your business's online presence. Lean into making informed decisions quickly to address emerging challenges. Balance short-term actions with long-term goals. Involve your team in decision-making processes to gain diverse perspectives and foster a sense of ownership.

Case Study: Turning Crisis into Opportunity - The Story of Jessica Scales

Jessica Scales, a single mother of two, founded a small handmade jewelry business, "Elegance by Jessica," in 2015. Her business quickly gained a loyal customer base due to her unique designs and individualized touch. However, in 2020, the COVID-19 pandemic hit, leading to a sharp decline in sales as physical stores closed and markets vanished overnight. The pandemic posed a significant threat to Jessica's livelihood. With two young children to support and her business income plummeting, she faced immense pressure. Despite the uncertainty, Jessica decided to confront the crisis head-on.

Jessica assessed the impact of the pandemic on her business and realized the need to shift her sales online. She activated her crisis management plan, focusing on digital transformation. She communicated transparently with her customers through social media and email newsletters, explaining the situation and her plans to transition to an online store. Jessica quickly learned the basics of e-commerce and digital marketing. She created an online store using platforms like Shopify and invested in learning about SEO and social media advertising.

Embracing a growth mindset, Jessica viewed the crisis as an opportunity to innovate and expand her business. She attended online courses on e-commerce and digital marketing to enhance her skills. Jessica leveraged technology to streamline her operations. She used project management tools to organize her tasks and automated her marketing campaigns using AI-driven tools. She engaged her customers through virtual events, live streams, and personalized email campaigns. By sharing behind-the-scenes stories and new product launches, she maintained customer interest and loyalty.

Deliberately think about what crisis you are currently facing and write it out:

_____

_____

_____

_____

_____

What are the 2 things you can do to leverage technology to avert the crisis from impeding your growth or scaling in the short term and long term?

_____

_____

_____

_____

Jessica used the downtime to innovate. She introduced new product lines, such as customizable jewelry that customers could design online. This personalized approach attracted new customers. With her newfound digital skills, Jessica expanded her reach beyond local markets. She utilized social media ads and influencer partnerships to target a global audience. Jessica joined online entrepreneurial communities where she shared her experiences and gained valuable insights. She also received support from mentors who guided her through the digital transition.

By the end of 2020, "Elegance by Jessica" had not only recovered from the initial impact of the pandemic but had also achieved record sales. Jessica's resilience and adaptability turned a crisis into a catalyst for growth. Her business model evolved, and she built a stronger, more sustainable business with a global customer base.

As a single parent entrepreneur, you have the inherent strength, resilience, and adaptability to navigate crises and turn challenges into opportunities. By preparing for potential crises, managing them effectively when they arise, and building resilience and adaptability, you can steer your business through tough times and emerge stronger.

Remember, crises are an inevitable part of the entrepreneurial journey, but they also offer opportunities for growth and innovation. Embrace each challenge with confidence and courage, knowing that your unique experiences and perspectives equip you to succeed. Jessica Scales' story serves as an inspiring example of what's possible when you face adversity head-on and leverage it to transform your business. Your journey, too, holds the potential for incredible success and impact. Keep moving forward, stay resilient, and let each crisis become a steppingstone to greater achievements.

Source:
Jessica Scales' story was featured in Forbes magazine's "Innovative Entrepreneurs of 2020" series, highlighting her successful pivot during the COVID-19 pandemic.

SECTION 4

CHAPTER 10: THE LEGACY

As a single parent entrepreneur, your journey is about more than just business success; it's about creating a legacy that transcends generations. Legacy building is the process of establishing a lasting impact that benefits not only your family and business but also your community and the broader world. It's about leaving a mark that endures long after you've stepped away from the day-to-day operations of your enterprise. This chapter will explore what it means to build a legacy, the strategies to achieve it, and real-life examples of entrepreneurs who have successfully created enduring legacies.

Legacy building is rooted in the values, vision, and mission that guide your entrepreneurial journey. It involves. Visionary Leadership is doing the work of curating a clear, compelling vision that inspires and guides others. Operating with integrity, transparency, and a commitment to social responsibility. Making meaningful contributions to the community and fostering a culture of giving back. Implementing practices that ensure the long-term viability of your business and its positive impact on the environment.

Building a legacy requires thoughtful planning and strategic actions. Here are key strategies to help you create a lasting impact: Start by envisioning the legacy you want to leave behind. Write down your legacy vision and use it as a guiding star for all your business decisions and actions. Consider the following questions.

- What values and principles do you want your business to embody?

- How do you want to be remembered by your family, employees, customers, and community?

- What long-term impact do you want your business to have on society and the environment?

A strong organizational culture is the foundation of a legacy. Cultivate a culture that reflects your values and promotes. Encourage honesty, transparency, and ethical behavior at all levels of the organization. Foster a culture of continuous improvement and innovation. Promote diversity, equity, and inclusion to create a welcoming and supportive environment for all employees. Invest in employee development and create opportunities for them to grow and thrive. A loyal, motivated workforce will carry your legacy forward.

Sustainable growth is key to building a legacy that endures. Develop a strategic plan that focuses on long-term goals rather than short-term gains. Use resources efficiently and responsibly to ensure the longevity of your business. Implement eco-friendly practices to minimize your business's environmental footprint. By prioritizing sustainability, you ensure that your business can continue to thrive and make a positive impact for years to come.

Engage with your community and make meaningful contributions. Support local charities, nonprofits, and community initiatives through donations, sponsorships, or volunteer efforts. Implement programs that address social issues relevant to your community, such as education, healthcare, or economic development. Collaborate with other businesses, community organizations, and government agencies to create positive change. Community engagement not only enhances your business's reputation but also strengthens the bonds between your business and the people it serves.

Document your journey, achievements, and lessons learned. Create a written history of your business that highlights key milestones and contributions. Share stories that capture the essence of your business's impact and the values that drive it. Mentor the next generation of entrepreneurs, passing on your knowledge and experiences to help them succeed. Sharing your legacy ensures that your story and values continue to inspire others long after you've moved on.

Case Study: Patagonia – A Legacy of Environmental Stewardship

Patagonia is a prime example of a business that has built a legacy through its commitment to environmental stewardship and social responsibility. Founded by Yvon Chouinard in 1973, Patagonia has become a leading outdoor apparel company known for its sustainable practices and advocacy for environmental causes.

Yvon Chouinard's vision was to create a company that not only produced high-quality outdoor gear but also championed environmental conservation. This vision has guided Patagonia's business practices and corporate culture from the very beginning.

Patagonia operates with a strong commitment to ethical business practices. The company uses organic cotton, recycled materials, and sustainable manufacturing processes to reduce its environmental impact. Additionally, Patagonia is transparent about its supply chain and works to ensure fair labor practices.

Patagonia actively engages with its community and supports environmental initiatives. The company donates 1% of its sales to environmental causes through its "1% for the Planet" program. Patagonia also encourages its employees to participate in environmental activism and provides grants to grassroots environmental organizations.

Patagonia's commitment to sustainability extends to all aspects of its business. The company has implemented initiatives such as the "Worn Wear" program, which encourages customers to repair, reuse, and recycle their Patagonia gear. By promoting a circular economy, Patagonia reduces waste and conserves resources.

As a single parent entrepreneur, you have the power to create a legacy that inspires and benefits future generations. By defining your legacy vision, building a strong organizational culture, focusing on sustainable growth, engaging with your community, and documenting your journey, you can ensure that your impact endures.

Remember, legacy building is not about achieving perfection but about making a positive difference. Each step you take towards creating a lasting impact, no matter how small, contributes to your legacy. Embrace the journey with passion, purpose, and perseverance, knowing that the values and principles you instill in your business will continue to inspire and influence others.

Your legacy is a testament to your hard work, dedication, and the love you have for your family, your business, and your community. As you continue to navigate the challenges and triumphs of entrepreneurship, keep your legacy vision at the forefront, and let it guide you towards creating a lasting and meaningful impact.

What legacy do you hope to leave through your entrepreneurial pursuits?

_____

_____

_____

_____

_____

_____

_____

CHAPTER 11: THE FUTURE

Single parent entrepreneurs are redefining entrepreneurship with their unique blend of resilience, creativity, and determination. As the world rapidly evolves, latest trends and opportunities are emerging, providing fertile ground for entrepreneurial growth. This chapter explores these emerging trends, prepares you for future challenges and innovations, and offers expert predictions to help you navigate the future with confidence and inspiration.

The COVID-19 pandemic accelerated the shift towards remote work, and this trend is here to stay. For single parent entrepreneurs, the rise of remote work offers unparalleled flexibility, enabling you to balance business responsibilities with family life more effectively. Remote work allows you to hire talent from around the world, diversifying your team and bringing in fresh perspectives. Operating a remote business can reduce overhead costs associated with physical office spaces. Flexible work arrangements help you better manage your time, reducing stress and increasing productivity. According to a Gartner survey, 74% of CFOs plan to shift some employees to remote work permanently, indicating that this trend will continue to grow.

Digital transformation is not just a buzzword; it's a necessity for staying competitive in today's market. Technologies like cloud computing, AI, and data analytics are revolutionizing how businesses operate. Automate routine tasks, allowing you to focus on strategic decision-making. Use data analytics to understand customer behavior and tailor your offerings. Digital tools enable you to scale your business operations seamlessly. A report by McKinsey & Company states that companies accelerated the digitization of their customer and supply-chain interactions by three to four years during the pandemic.

The e-commerce sector has seen exponential growth, driven by changing consumer behaviors and technological advancements. For single parent entrepreneurs, e-commerce presents a lucrative opportunity to reach a broader audience without the constraints of a physical storefront. Online platforms enable you to sell products and services to customers worldwide. Starting an online business requires less capital compared to traditional retail. Utilize e-commerce analytics to optimize inventory, pricing, and marketing strategies. According to Statista, global e-commerce sales are projected to reach $6.54 trillion by 2023, underscoring the immense potential of this market.

Consumers are increasingly prioritizing sustainability and social responsibility when making purchasing decisions. Businesses that align with these values can build strong, loyal customer bases. Stand out in the market by committing to sustainable practices. Attract and retain customers who value ethical and environmentally friendly businesses. Contribute to social and environmental causes, enhancing your brand's reputation. A Nielsen report found that 66% of global consumers are willing to pay more for sustainable brands, highlighting the importance of sustainability in business strategy.

The pace of technological change is relentless. Staying ahead requires continuous learning and adaptation. Embrace innovative technologies and integrate them into your business model to remain competitive. Keep up with industry news and trends through reputable sources and professional networks. Provide ongoing education and training for yourself and your team to stay current with technological advancements. Be open to experimenting with new tools and approaches and learn from both successes and failures.

Economic fluctuations are inevitable, and being prepared can help you weather financial storms. Develop strategies to ensure your business remains resilient in the face of economic challenges. Reduce dependence on a sole source of income by exploring multiple revenue channels. Maintain a reserve fund to manage cash flow during tough times. Stay vigilant about economic indicators and adjust your business strategies accordingly.

Innovation is key to staying relevant and competitive. Encourage a culture of creativity and continuous improvement within your business. Encourage your team to share ideas and experiment with innovative solutions. Partner with other businesses, startups, or academic institutions to drive innovation. Use customer insights to guide product development and service enhancements.

AI and machine learning are expected to play an increasingly significant role in business operations. These technologies can help automate tasks, provide predictive insights, and enhance customer interactions. By 2025, AI will be integral to various business functions, from marketing and customer service to supply chain management and decision-making. Companies that effectively harness AI will gain a substantial competitive edge. A report by PwC predicts that AI could contribute up to $15.7 trillion to the global economy by 2030, with productivity gains and innovation being key drivers.

Personalization will become a cornerstone of customer engagement. Businesses that deliver tailored experiences will see higher customer satisfaction and loyalty. Advances in data analytics and AI will enable hyper-personalized marketing, where businesses can anticipate and respond to individual customer needs in real-time. According to Salesforce, 84% of customers say being treated like a person, not a number, is especially important to winning their business.

The gig economy will continue to expand, providing flexible work opportunities and reshaping traditional employment models. By 2025, the gig economy will encompass a sizable portion of the workforce, with more businesses relying on freelance and contract workers for specialized tasks and projects. A study by Mastercard estimated that the global gig economy generated $455 billion in annual revenue in 2023.

As awareness of mental health issues grows, businesses will place greater emphasis on employee wellbeing. This focus will not only improve workplace culture but also enhance productivity and employee retention. By 2025, mental health and wellbeing programs will be standard practice in businesses, driven by both ethical considerations and the need to attract and retain top talent. The World Health Organization predicts that mental health conditions will be the leading cause of disability by 2030, underscoring the importance of proactive mental health strategies.

The future of single parent entrepreneurship is bright, filled with exciting opportunities and transformative trends. By staying informed, adaptable, and innovative, you can navigate the evolving business landscape with confidence and success. Embrace the flexibility offered by remote work, harness the power of digital transformation, and tap into the growing e-commerce market. Prioritize sustainability and social responsibility to build a brand that resonates with modern consumers. Prepare for future challenges by continuously learning, diversifying revenue streams, and fostering a culture of innovation.

As a single parent entrepreneur, your journey is marked by resilience and determination. Leverage these strengths to seize new opportunities and overcome obstacles. The insights and predictions shared in this chapter are meant to guide and inspire you, ensuring that you are well-equipped to thrive in the dynamic world of entrepreneurship. The future is yours to shape. With courage, vision, and an unwavering commitment to your goals, you can redefine what it means to be an entrepreneur and leave a legacy for yourself and your family. Remember, the challenges you face are not barriers but steppingstones to greater success. Embrace the future with confidence and watch your entrepreneurial dreams come to life.

References

1. Gartner. (2020). "74% of CFOs plan to shift some employees to remote work permanently." Retrieved from [Gartner](https://www.gartner.com).
2. McKinsey & Company. (2020). "How COVID-19 has pushed companies over the technology tipping point." Retrieved from [McKinsey & Company] (https://www.mckinsey.com).
3. Statista. (2020). "Global e-commerce sales are projected to reach $6.54 trillion by 2023." Retrieved from [Statista](https://www.statista.com).
4. Nielsen. (2018). "Consumers are willing to pay more for sustainable brands." Retrieved from [Nielsen](https://www.nielsen.com).
5. PwC. (2018). "AI to drive GDP gains of $15.7 trillion by 2030." Retrieved from [PwC](https://www.pwc.com).
6. Salesforce. (2019). "State of the Connected Customer." Retrieved from [Salesforce](https://www.salesforce.com).
7. Mastercard. (2019). "The Global Gig Economy: Capitalizing on a ~$500B Opportunity." Retrieved from [Mastercard](https://www.mastercard.com).
8. World Health Organization. (2020). "Mental health conditions to be the leading cause of disability by 2030." Retrieved from [WHO](https://www.who.int).

CHAPTER 12: THE ETHICS

As you embrace AI, it's essential to consider the ethical implications. Use AI responsibly, ensuring that your practices align with ethical standards and regulations. Protect customer data and privacy and be transparent about how you use AI in your business. Implement robust data security measures to protect sensitive information. Use AI tools that comply with data protection regulations and prioritize customer privacy. Building trust with your customers is paramount, and responsible AI use can enhance your reputation. Be transparent about how you use AI in your business operations. Ensure that AI algorithms are fair and unbiased, avoiding discrimination and promoting inclusivity. Ethical AI practices can strengthen your brand's integrity and foster customer loyalty.

Your journey as a single parent entrepreneur leveraging AI can inspire others to pursue their entrepreneurial dreams. Share your experiences, mentor aspiring entrepreneurs, and contribute to a supportive community. Offer guidance and support to other single parent entrepreneurs. Share your knowledge about AI and its applications, helping them navigate their entrepreneurial journey with confidence. Engage with entrepreneurial communities, both online and offline. Participate in forums, attend conferences, and contribute to discussions about AI and entrepreneurship. By actively participating in these communities, you can expand your network and stay updated on the latest trends.

Advocate for the adoption of AI among small businesses and single parent entrepreneurs. Educate others about the benefits and practical applications of AI, empowering them to embrace technology and drive their businesses forward. As a single parent entrepreneur, you are already a beacon of strength and resilience. By embracing AI, you can elevate your business, achieve peak performance, and create a legacy that inspires others.

AI is not just a tool; it's a transformative force that can help you overcome challenges, seize opportunities, and redefine what it means to be an entrepreneur. Step into the future with confidence, knowing that you have the power to harness AI to its fullest potential.

Be sure you have a written policy for how, when, where, and why you are using AI for your business. Be clear in your approach and expectations of the influence of AI in your systems and processes. Explicitly explain your stance on the ethics of AI implementation currently an as advances come so there is no room for error or confusion. Business owners often have a policy and workflow in place for the use of technology as it relates to laptops and cellphones, but not the use of platforms like chatbots and data collection. Don't be that person. Be the leader that is courageous enough to speak on AI and how will be used in your business.

Your journey is a testament to the limitless possibilities that arise when courage, determination, and technology converge. Embrace AI, and let it propel you toward unparalleled success and fulfillment. The world is waiting for your unique brilliance—go out and shine! You are courageous!

When did you or will you have a written AI policy in your corporate operations files?

CHAPTER 13: THE QUESTIONS

Taking time to seriously reflect without interruptions, outside influences or mental obstacles can help you focus your energy and actions. Here are key questions you should take the time to ask yourself to help open your eyes and mind to grow your business while leveraging AI technology and applications:

1. Market and Customer Understanding
    - Who are my target customers and what are their pain points?
    - How can I use AI to better understand and predict my customers' needs and preferences?
    - What data do I need to collect to improve customer segmentation and personalization?

2. Product and Service Enhancement
    - How can AI help me improve the quality or efficiency of my products/services?
    - Are there AI-driven innovations in my industry that I can adopt to stay competitive?

3. Operational Efficiency
    - Which of my current processes can be automated using AI to save time and reduce costs?
    - How can AI improve my inventory management and supply chain coordination?

4. Marketing and Sales
    - What AI tools can help me optimize my marketing campaigns and increase my reach?
    - How can AI assist in lead generation and conversion to boost my sales?

5. Customer Service
- Can AI-powered chatbots or virtual assistants enhance my customer service experience?
- How can I use AI to gather and analyze customer feedback for continuous improvement?

6. Financial Management
- Are there AI solutions that can help me with financial planning and forecasting?
- How can I use AI to better manage cash flow and identify potential financial risks?

7. Time Management
- What AI tools can help me better manage my time and prioritize tasks effectively?
- How can AI assist in creating a more balanced work-life schedule?

8. Learning and Development
- What AI resources are available for upskilling myself and my team?
- How can I stay updated on the latest AI trends and technologies relevant to my business?

9. Scalability and Growth
- How can AI support my plans for scaling my business?
- What AI-driven insights can help identify new market opportunities or expansion strategies?

10. Data Privacy and Security
- How can I ensure that my use of AI complies with data privacy regulations?
- What measures should I take to protect my business and customer data from cyber threats?

11. Collaboration and Networking
- Are there AI platforms that can help me connect with potential partners, mentors, or investors?

- How can AI facilitate better communication and collaboration within my team?
-

12. Sustainability and Ethics
    - How can AI help me make my business more sustainable and environmentally friendly?
    - What ethical considerations should I keep in mind when implementing AI solutions in my business?

Invest your time now in answering the questions with sincerity and honesty. Get a good gauge as to where you are now, but don't stop there. By regularly reflecting on these questions, you can strategically leverage AI to grow your business while managing your unique challenges and responsibilities. This is an ongoing process of reflection, evolution, and responsibility.

_____

_____

_____

_____

_____

_____

_____

_____

_____

SECTION 5

CHAPTER 14: THE SINGULARITY

As we come to the concluding chapter of this walk into the possibilities of the future, it's essential to reflect on the incredible path you've traveled. Whether you're in the initial stages of your entrepreneurial adventure or already running a thriving business, your determination and resilience as a single parent entrepreneur are truly remarkable. This chapter aims to inspire continued growth and perseverance while encouraging you to take the next step in your entrepreneurial journey. With heartfelt gratitude, I share these final words of encouragement.

You have taken on one of the most challenging and rewarding roles imaginable: balancing the demands of parenthood with the responsibilities of entrepreneurship. This dual role requires a unique blend of skills, including time management, strategic thinking, and emotional intelligence. Embrace these strengths as the foundation of your success.

The truth is your personal journey as a single parent has undoubtedly tested your resilience. The challenges you've faced have strengthened your ability to bounce back from setbacks and adapt to new situations. This resilience is a powerful asset in the business world, where change is constant, and obstacles are inevitable. Trust in your capacity to overcome challenges and view each hurdle as an opportunity for growth.

As a parent, empathy is second nature. It's one of your many superpowers. This ability to understand and share the feelings of others is invaluable in business. It allows you to connect with your team, understand your customers' needs, and build strong relationships. Use this empathy to create a supportive and inclusive business environment that fosters collaboration and innovation.

Your vision is the driving force behind your entrepreneurial journey. It is what motivates you to keep going, even when the road is tough. Keep your vision at the forefront of everything you do. Let it guide your decisions, inspire your actions, and remind you of your purpose. In the face of challenges and distractions, it can be easy to lose sight of your original vision.

Stay true to your vision, and let it serve as your North Star. Your vision is unique, and it is what sets you apart from others. Believe in it wholeheartedly and let it guide you towards success. While it's important to stay true to your vision, be open to adapting and evolving. The business landscape is constantly changing, and flexibility is key to staying relevant. Embrace change and use it as an opportunity to refine and enhance your vision. Remember, evolution is a sign of growth.

The road forward for an entrepreneur is one of continuous learning and growth. Embrace this path with a mindset of curiosity and a willingness to learn. Your greatest asset is you. Invest in your personal and professional development by seeking out new knowledge, skills, and experiences. Attending workshops, reading books, taking courses, and seeking mentorship. The more you learn, the more equipped you will be to navigate the complexities of entrepreneurship.

Challenges are inevitable, but they are also opportunities for growth. Each challenge you face is a chance to learn something new and develop new skills. Approach challenges with a positive mindset and view them as steppingstones towards your goals.

No journey is meant to be traveled alone. Building a dedicated support network is crucial for your success and well-being. Mentorship can provide valuable guidance, support, and insights. Find mentors who have walked a similar path and can offer advice based on their experiences. Their wisdom and perspective can help you navigate challenges and make informed decisions.

Surround yourself with people who believe in you and your vision. Positive and supportive relationships can provide encouragement, motivation, and a sense of community. Lean on your friends and family for emotional support and engage with entrepreneurial communities where you can share experiences and learn from others.

As a single parent and entrepreneur, it's easy to prioritize the needs of your family and business above your own. However, self-care is crucial for your well-being and effectiveness as a leader. Your well-being has implications for the well-being of the people around you and the business you are building. Make it a priority. Take care of your physical health by maintaining a balanced diet, getting regular exercise, and ensuring adequate sleep. Your physical well-being directly impacts your energy levels, focus, and productivity. Pay attention to your mental and emotional health. Practice mindfulness, meditation, or other stress-relief techniques. Seek professional help if needed. Remember, taking care of your mental health is not a sign of weakness but a strength. Establish boundaries to ensure a healthy work-life balance. Allocate time for yourself, your family, and your business. Protect your personal time and avoid overworking. A well-balanced life will enable you to perform at your best.

Take the time to celebrate your achievements, no matter how small they may seem. Each milestone is a testament to your hard work, dedication, and perseverance. You are making progress by reading this book and doing the work to understand what AI is and how to apply it to your growth and development. Reflect on how far you've come and the progress you've made. Acknowledge the effort and sacrifices you've invested in your journey. Celebrating your achievements boosts morale and provides motivation to keep moving forward. Share your successes with your support network. Celebrating with others strengthens your relationships and provides additional encouragement. Your achievements can also inspire others who are on a similar journey.

Your journey as a single parent entrepreneur serves as a powerful example for your children and others in your community. You are showing them the values of hard work, resilience, and the pursuit of dreams. Demonstrate the qualities you wish to instill in your children and others around you. Show them the importance of perseverance, integrity, and dedication. Your actions speak louder than words and will leave an impression. Encourage your children to dream big and pursue their passions. Support their interests and provide them with opportunities to explore and learn. Your journey can inspire them to believe in themselves and their potential.

As this chapter ends, I encourage you to take the next step in your entrepreneurial journey with confidence and determination. Reflect on your vision and set new goals for the future. Whether it's expanding your business, launching a new product, or entering a new market, set clear and achievable goals that align with your vision. Action is the key to progress. Take the first step towards your new goals, no matter how small it may be. Each step forward brings you closer to your vision.

Embrace the experience with a positive mindset and a willingness to learn. Stay connected with your support network and seek out new opportunities for growth and learning. Engage with communities, attend events, and build relationships with like-minded individuals. Your network is a valuable resource for support, inspiration, and collaboration. As you continue to grow and succeed, find ways to give back to your community. Share your knowledge, mentor others, and support causes that are important to you. Giving back enriches your journey and creates a positive impact on others.

To the single parent entrepreneur reading this, I want to express my heartfelt gratitude. Your life is a source of inspiration and strength. Your determination and resilience remind us that anything is possible with hard work, dedication, and an unobstructed vision. Thank you for allowing me to be a part of your journey. It has been an honor to share these insights and words of encouragement with you. I believe in your potential and am confident that you will achieve remarkable things.

You are a testament to how a person can have incredible strength, resilience, and determination. Embrace your unique path, believe in your vision, and trust in your abilities. Continue to learn, grow, and build dedicated support networks. Prioritize your well-being and celebrate your achievements.

As you move forward, remember that you are not alone. Countless others have walked this path and emerged stronger and more successful. You have the power to achieve greatness and create a legacy. Embrace your journey with confidence and courage and know that you are capable of extraordinary things.

With heartfelt gratitude and sincere encouragement, I wish you continued success and real fulfillment on your entrepreneurial journey. The world needs more courageous leaders like you. Thank you, and may your journey be filled with exponential growth, good success, and endless possibilities.

THE AUTHOR'S STORY

Dionne Marie Flynn, the visionary Founder and CEO of Dionne Marie Signature Haute Ventures, is a hopeful and experienced entrepreneur. She's a catalyst for transformation in the luxury market. With a dynamic blend of expertise in peak performance development, leadership strategy cultivation, and international corporate compliance, Ambassador Flynn delivers more than just strategies – she delivers breakthroughs.

Known as the "Luxe Ambassador," Ambassador Flynn is renowned for her unparalleled ability to elevate mindsets, unpack pain points, and align language with expectations. Her mission? To empower one million leaders worldwide to reach their optimum performance by bridging the gap between spiritual development and professional acumen.

With over two decades of experience in ministry, the legal field and the government, Ambassador Flynn's journey from a first-generation immigrant to a global influencer is nothing short of inspirational. Leveraging her background in ministry leadership, executive management, and support roles in government, corporations, law firms, and universities, she draws from a rich tapestry of experiences to mentor the next generation of emerging leaders.

A lifelong learner, Ambassador Flynn has curated a non-traditional academic path, accentuating her C-Suite leadership development with multiple certifications in Lean Six Sigma, Global Trade and Logistics, Corporate Governance, and more. Currently pursuing her studies at Harvard University with a focus on strategy development, she embodies the ethos of continual growth and advancement.

As an ordained minister and humanitarian, Ambassador Flynn's commitment to empowering individuals extends beyond the boardroom. She is an innovative ministry leader. She was licensed in 2001 to preach the gospel by Bishop Joseph Simmons, ordained and affirmed as a Pastor in 2008 by Bishop TD Jakes, and later elevated to the office of Overseer in 2010. She enjoys traveling across the globe speaking life to leaders. From serving as a Liaison for the International Law Section of the American Bar Association to supporting international trade as a goodwill trade ambassador, she exemplifies compassionate leadership with a global perspective.

Approachable, compassionate, and deeply committed to improving human performance, Ambassador Flynn balances her executive responsibilities with her role as a devoted mother of two young adults. With a passion for languages, vegan dining adventures, and a childhood in St. Croix and Harlem, NY, her journey is as diverse and vibrant as the clients she serves.

Intrigued? Contact Ambassador Flynn while on your journey of empowerment, enlightenment, and excellence – where every interaction is not just a conversation, but a catalyst for positive change.

@msdionnemarie
info@dmshaute.ventures
www.dmshaute.ventures

www.ingramcontent.com/pod-product-compliance
Lightning Source LLC
Chambersburg PA
CBHW071835210526
45479CB00001B/149